our place on earth

our place on earth

vic lejon

for my younger self

people ask me
what justifies
our place on earth

but i cannot
answer

a human's
purpose
is a choice

mine
lies
in my voice

stolen
for years
i took it back

to allow
my words
to be alive

- our place on earth

our place on earth

contents

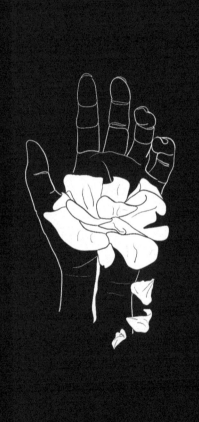

chapter I

hearts crumble and grow anew
the same way wild roses do

i gave away
my beating heart
to show people
i love them

but people lose
and break things
fill up boxes
with memorabilia
toss them in the attic

it is a war zone up there
armies of forgotten hearts
torture and terrorise the past

i have learnt my lesson
come find my love here
on these pages
instead

read about it
if you want to
burn it down
if we are no more

just do not take
my heart from me
i need it

- sacrifice

our place on earth

wherever you go
hearts soften

without permission
or encouragement
my heart unfurled
from the shy bud
it had been
cocooned in

waiting for the right
moment
person
time
took too long

it began to fight
and struggle
causing a ruckus
amongst the other organs
who thought it was in revolt

all it wanted
was to bloom
for itself

- blossoming

our place on earth

the air
exhaled
when we met
beneath
the sand sculptures
by the sea

your baritone
singing voice
pulled me in

you said
my smile
was the brightest beam
you had ever
seen

        - opal dreams

vic lejon

my auntie
used to say

when you meet
the right person
there will be
moments
during which
neither of you
speak

yet
their breath
and your breath
hold all the words
you need

- when breaths become voices

our place on earth

the autumn leaves
fall silently
in love
with your green eyes

   - *falling*

vic lejon

we bathe in
liquid moonbeams
gently gliding
down our spines

like warm honey
on cold marble
quivering bodies
blooming minds

we move
like we own
the world
at night

- midnight gold

our place on earth

limbs
pressed together

sunshine
soaked the room

the softest falling
i ever lived through

　　- morning hours

that morning
you whispered
about
oceans
pretending
to be eyes

as if a human being
could ever
epitomise
a force of nature

you said
if anyone could
it would be
me

and i rolled
my blue eyes
at your womanising
poetry

- smooth sailing

our place on earth

i play
love songs
through
an open window
and the moon
beams
happily

    - lunar infatuation

you gifted me
the pieces
the ones
before me
already knew

their
fingerprints
and lipstick
their hands
all over you

i want
the parts
you keep hidden
locked in a treasure chest
at the bottom
of the sea

will you
trust me?

- unprecedented depth

our place on earth

it was the honeymoon phase
and you yawned
violently

your body spread
on my bed
like you
owned it
not me

we should go somewhere,
you suggested

sure

how about we chase
those lights you like?

the northern lights, i hummed
not quite listening

i was captivated by rainbow prisms
glittering on your skin

- dancing lights

when you read
my poems and
they are about
you

words will turn
into wildflowers
and tumble
to your feet

- can i trust you?

our place on earth

i am just here
breathing
but i wish to be
with you
loving

- displaced

there was a night
that broke us
it haunts my
memory

messy hair
glazed eyes
smeared lipstick
on your face

you were late, mumbling
about lost soul mates
told me to trust you
held me in your embrace

and i dragged you
down the street
towards the sleeping sea
to get lost in a starry-eyed
fantasy

from the start
we walked on
that fine line
between perfection
and catastrophe

- fatal

our place on earth

i am impaled
at the height
of your deceit

my heart
heaves
quietly

i never
wanted to
see

your face
on the red flag
smiling down
at me

- *warning signs*

vic lejon

the churning
of concrete
has replaced
daily cooking

our passive aggression
shovels substances into
our throats to fill the gaps
we allowed to grow

scrape
slap
mould us
to perfection

live in this routine
accept the tall stories
set them in stone
commemorate comfort zones

but
do i like you?
do i like me?

no
not anymore
not at all, actually

- let's pretend we're fine

our place on earth

i throw up
dead butterflies
wash my mouth
dab my lips
pretend to smile

when my friends ask,
what's wrong?

i lie

   - it's complicated

vic lejon

why
couldn't i
see the light
everyone told me
to find
inside myself
(after you left)

all this time
i was buried
in your heart
not living
with mine

and what
remained
of us
was the dust
of crushed opals
on the finish line

- *we are broken*

our place on earth

i keep missing
the exit
on my way home
to the person
i used to be

i am stuck
wearing
this shell
of a woman
i do not recognise
as me

- stranger in the rear-view mirror

vic lejon

i was a play
to you
a piece of art
on a stage

in the clothes
you put on me
with the smile
you gave me
after a night
full of games

i did not know
you just liked directing

you liked the reaction
from the audience

you liked what you saw
of yourself in me
not the woman i became

- it's all made-up

our place on earth

shower me
in moonlight
i am only
skin and bones

hold me
in the darkness
and you will feel
my soul

- trueness

vic lejon

you spooned out
my chest cavity
put it
into a blender
poured it
into a glass

stir me
stir me up
baby

i am a wholesome breakfast
you lead the healthy lifestyle

(i am too giving
i know that now)

scooped and hollowed
gasping for air
i have nowhere
to go

i am a human being
without a blood flow

  - *toxic smoothie*

our place on earth

the sound
of coins
falling
onto the parquet
woke the flowers
in the living-room

the peonies
they growled
saw through you
from the start

their petals
became projectiles
the red roses
raised their thorns

leave your change
in the hallway, human,
along with your mask

- the softest protectors

vic lejon

i decant
tears
like you do
with wine

to separate
what is
yours
and what is
mine

i do not want
to infuse my future
with someone
i no longer like

- *sediment*

our place on earth

do not compare me
to the moon
or the sun
or the stars

i am an entire galaxy
black hole
and all its parts

too much for you
to handle

too far for you
to grasp

- galactic

vic lejon

you said
i am the ocean

you were right
(at least this once)

the seven seas
roar inside of me

my waves surge
and erode

no rip-rap
can save you
(green eyes)

i will never stop
to flow

      - overflow

gold threads
hold my heart
where others
gripped
and ripped
for so long

plague-ridden
promises
and pretentious
love poems
have only
made it
glow
stronger

> - *kintsugi*
> *(golden repair, Japanese)*

vic lejon

he
she
they all feel
the same
to me

am i deserving
of more?

you made me
question it

and i empty
the bottles
of self-love
i had stored
in the back
of my closet

out of your sight
out of my mind

they smell
rotten
now

- *moving on*

our place on earth

i write about love
every day

but if you
stopped me
in the street

and asked me
to define what
love means

i would not
say a word

too scared
vulnerability
might creep
out

    - love is scary

the heart is the most stubborn
creature i know

our place on earth

a plane was
my escape
from home

it could have been
a boat
but you liked those
and i no longer liked
you

still, thoughts
about you
pester me
when i want to sleep

make me question
the identity
i built
for myself

who is this girl
in the mirror
always choking
on quicksand

since we split
i have crash-landed
in a stranger's reality
(mine)

vic lejon

every morning over coffee
i have to remind my heart
that we are alone
it will be okay

it is the old me
who misses
the tears

it is the new me
who wants to explore
the untrodden ways

tugged between book stores
and tea-scented walls
lies a whole new world

i think you will like it there,
i tell my heart

i only like him, it says
but my heart has no choice
it has to mend its ways
with time, life will be better

i am no longer a free sample
for everyone to squeeze and taste,
my heart proclaims one day,
hope and freedom is what
i pump

our place on earth

i travel on the edge
of tectonic plates
now

stand on top of mountains
murder self-doubts
and dress
how i like now

my soul is fierce
and my heart
space
free of you

embracing
the healing

free-falling
in the sky

i am learning
to pry open
my own wings

no longer in need of anyone
i only need myself to fly

- on my own

chapter II

minds can be heaven and hell
at the same time

vic lejon

a moth flutters
against my window
at 3.45

its wings
finger paint
a skull on the glass

another visit
from my friend, death

leave me alone
my skin is too busy
to shiver in fear

it is attempting
to unzip itself
and walk away

the moth
it is a distraction

despite darkening
prospects of sanctuary
it wants to come inside

a smattering of light
is a more hopeful place
than all-consuming darkness

- lessons from the mundane

our place on earth

some days
no matter
what i eat
i feel like i am
chewing bullets

metallic ecstasy

unfired explosives
sleep
and leech
off my tongue

i add
cinnamon sticks
and soak them
in holy water

the bullets
they laugh

they smoke
cigarettes
like warlords do

- occupied territory

vic lejon

a little kid
told me
she could not wait
to start school

it made me reminisce
about the bad, old days

sobbing
in bathroom stalls
playing hostess
to panic and anxiety

the day i learnt
depression is real
and so is suicide
but never learnt
to seek help

and
i hoped
for this kindergartner
she would be smarter than i

- education

when the soul is wild
but the mind is tired
that is when we struggle
to be kind to ourselves

- the importance of self-care

vic lejon

they tell me
i have nice hair

porcelain skin
perfect teeth

what a friendly soul
composed and calm

i nod my head
in thanks

if only they knew
about the carnage inside

- self-destructive tendency

our place on earth

let me open
my body
to show you

these
shredded
velveteen bones
and self-inflicted
wounds

so you can understand
you are not alone

(you are never alone)

there are many of us
and you will find your way too

- everyone is afraid

vic lejon

trauma, heartbreak
and death catch you
at the unexpected
times

they want to bend
your backbone

flush out the personality
that made you you

your old pieces
will no longer fit

some will fracture
become incompatible

they will force you
to build another you

it will be uncomfortable
your body and soul
will twinge and ache

but you will get there
you will find yourself
again

- puzzle pieces

there was no choice
in my tumultuous silence
no act of anger
or teenage defiance

my mind
stole my lips
in unsolicited
violence

snatched
from my face
but i stole them back

NOW

i choose when i speak
when that is my will

i control when i am mute
and when my words kill

- selective mutism

(selective mutism is a childhood anxiety disorder
that renders someone unable to speak in certain
social settings, for more information check out
selectivemutismcenter.org/)

vic lejon

they pried
my lips open
squeezed
their grimy
slimy
fingers
down my throat
till i choked

she *can* speak
why doesn't she?

- voice box controllers

our place on earth

a light beam
is trapped in
my chest

not a scatter
makes it out alive

yes
my heart is opaque
(do not question it)

focus on the light
it is searching for
a graze

at any moment
my heart could crack

unleash brilliance
and joy

how fragile it is
to be sad

- melancholy under threat

vic lejon

sadness looks different
on every face

there are seven billion
versions of a day

- reminder

i do not want
to glorify pain

i want you to know
you will get through it

    - trust in your strength

vic lejon

a constant falling and rising
in our lungs
the ocean
life

    - *in, out / up, down*

our place on earth

the neighbour's kid
tried to glue leaves
back onto trees

autumn thunders
never broke his will

they furthered
his motivation
to fix the broken
things

he knew

it does not
matter for
how long
you have blown
in the wind

or how strong
the rains beat
your skin

you can always
grow again

- *thunders*

everyone acts like they are in control.
let me find an excuse, let me play along
with your pretence.

i do not want you to think i struggle too.
there are no doubts, worries or fears
in my head. that's only you.

make-up, i don't need that.
is your skin not in perfect condition?
(i am sarcastic.)

i joke with the truth to cover the pain of
losing my mind last night. it happens a lot,
i'll tell you.

people believe the stories you spread for the
sake of conformity. ask them about their
hobbies. they will list their best traits.

they do not want you to think
they struggle to pull their own weight.

(the truth is they forgot to do the dishes
before they met you.)

their heads are already full of themselves.
(it's the dishes, they stack.) don't fear others'
judgements. we all pretend.

- *the contest*

our place on earth

i have not
been honest
with you

i am trying
to hide
i am weak
but all i do
is self-destruct

how does
lying to you
help me?

- let's be honest with each other

vic lejon

insecurities
lived on the silver spoons
in our house

we sucked them up
like honey
to learn

how to give up
how *not* to love people
how to lie to ourselves

these days
we are expected
to be better than you

- familial expectations

our place on earth

during my teenage years
i was doused in whiskey
and gasoline

to simplify
that lighter toss

perfect the efficiency
of self-destruction

(a simple flick of the wrist)

now i am happy
i never did

- *childhood monsters mature*

vic lejon

whenever we meet
you lash me with cruelty

hatred possesses your hands
you wring my neck

my tongue suffocates
turns black

falls from my mouth
in ashes

i know you hurt
your eyes cry

and i open my arms wide
to let my heart pour

kindness spills all over you

- empath

our place on earth

i am many things
and many
i am not

but i am
most definitely
resilient

          - *i am, i am, i am*

in the rivers of my soul
there are a million eyes

i dance
i cry
i heal
i break
but
i never die

- stages of being

our place on earth

the women
of this family
were born
into mental chaos

and they cry about
cursed genes
inherited trauma
insanity

it's
our minds
they hatch flames

it's
our hearts
they butcher
oceans

we underestimate
the powers we were
trusted with
by the women
before us

there is a space
between weakness
and strength

  - *potential*

vic lejon

the faults
we find in others
are often
fault lines
in our own
hearts

- *the shadow selves*

i like to name
my monsters

they lose
their frightening charm

and when i overcome them
i have something
to remember them by

- a book full of names

vic lejon

you will reach
a point of clarity
in your life

looking at
the never-ending skies
unimaginable mountains
across the deepest oceans

feeling
the heat of earth
pounding
like a giant heart
underneath your feet

you will understand
our existence
means nothing
and oddly
that is empowering

- mental landscapes

the biggest lie i told myself:
there is no other way

vic lejon

i write for souls
who do not have a home
who lost theirs
who are searching
who never found one

writing is my home
and i open my doors
to give you one too
even if it is just
a fleeting moment
i want you to feel safe
and know
whatever troubles you
it will pass

- lost and found

be cautious
of the pains
you allow
to reside
in your soul

   - shared spaces

vic lejon

everything takes
more time

walking
talking
breathing

the exertion
of being

when your mind
is sad

- *battling depression*

our place on earth

my mind devours
itself

it has done so
many times

over time
you learn
that killing
the bad thoughts
is not killing
you

> *- defeated monsters*
> *howl the loudest*

vic lejon

that cold, dark place
inside me has died

   - i still look for it
   (sometimes)

my soul has always
been wiser
than the mind
i possess

she is a
white-haired lady
knitting
in a rocking chair

while i am
mentally
crumbling
like parched petals

she remains
calm

planting
whispers
in my ears

your heart is beating
this is just a day
a moment in time
that is not worth it
to cause your life
dismay

   - old soul

vic lejon

there is nothing heroic
about a heart
detonating
in the dark

unable to beat
because sadness
has dressed it
in dynamite

the heroic part comes later
when the owner of said heart
finds a shred of hope
under their fingernail

grabs it, holds it tight
knuckles turn white
sweat breaks, tears fall
and the body rises
to remind you

life is horrific
but beautiful

you control the trigger
the heart is under
your ownership
as is your brain
you have all the tools
learn how to use them

- inside you

our place on earth

after every run-in
with sadness
i have to peel
the wet leaves
off my skin
to find
that happy girl
again

- sticky recovery

you have the strength
to become what you need

our place on earth

respect people's pain
you do not know
what they see

- a word on respect

vic lejon

take your convoluted feelings
and smear them
across a page

crimson and indigo
                    tears
          will begin to rearrange
                          into poetry

- *coping mechanism*

our place on earth

i was kneeling
in front of the *old me*
as if
she held power
as if
she was in control

you are not, i spat
and i rose

until her head
could tilt no more

i rose

until it threatened
to snap

i rose

towering above
who i used to be
i find my present
is wild and free
full of possibilities

- old me

vic lejon

i cannot always speak
when you want me to
(nor when i want to)

my mind tells my body
it is dangerous

the more you pressure me
the tighter you pull the noose
around my neck

- social anxiety

our place on earth

whoever told you
that strength is
strapping sadness
to your spine

carrying it with you
uphill and down
through rivers
deserts
snow
and sunshine

those are ancient lies
told by people
who did not know
better

the art of strength lies
in accepting emotions

learning
how to
let them go
when you need to

learning
to ask for help
when you need to

- everyone is learning

vic lejon

the terrorising thoughts
wielded me
into a weapon
not expecting me
to persist

now, i am in charge
and they should run

> *- once a little girl,*
> *now a warrior*

our place on earth

i see your monsters
and bite my tongue

they are not mine to battle
yet i turn around

i need to scream and shout
open my mouth
to ask what i can do

your monsters are familiar
let me help you
desiccate them

i know how
and i know how it feels
to chase them
on your own

- warrior souls

vic lejon

that's a handsome fellow
he's nice to look at
kind of a pretty boy,
they said

i glanced over
my shoulder
and knew
his stormy gaze
meant shame

an understanding
established us

(passersby in this busy world)

as kindred spirits
high on pain

   - *boys cry too*

our place on earth

dear self

i am sorry
for breaking you

i know it took you
years to fix the damage

i promise
i am learning to be gentler
it is more complicated than i thought

- patience

vic lejon

she walks a
sun-soaked path

apricot silk dresses
flowers and music

a house filled
with bustle and glee

her life must be perfect

and yet
she is drowning
inside

- appearances lie

our place on earth

it takes
brave souls
to find strength
in the broken

stripped
of all
society deems
alluring and confident

only the fragile
remain standing
when earth trembles

for they have been
trembling
all along

running
through this life
without armour
to protect their hearts

they will be there
to catch the strong
when they fall apart

- the importance of the fragile

vic lejon

i feel everything
is it good or bad?

i see details
in the complex
and the bland

i hear the things
you do not say
the things you lack

but i also hear
the song of love
and kindness

what a priceless
gift to have

- in tune with myself

our place on earth

we fall
and fly
so rapidly
there is no time
for us
to
be

- *highly-sensitive people*

vic lejon

melancholy is at home
in the chambers
of my heart

greeting
every blood cell
on its path

hi.
hello!
how are you today?

miserable?
wonderful!
have a glorious day.

- glorified mental illness

our place on earth

a light switch,
darkness

a last breath,
death

so much
can happen
in one second

    - silence

vic lejon

depression is a knife
held by an invisible hand

it cuts through muscles
and bones

you bleed liquid ice
instead of red

>   - *what does it feel like,*
>   *they ask*

our place on earth

i break
and beg
for someone
to save me

i am met
by brutal silence

we will help you,
they always say
(they never do)

then the plot twists
in my favour

heart, mind
and soul
grab me by
my shoulders
put me on my feet
wipe the dirt
from my knees

try again
just try
and i do

- self-reliance

shattered
into a billion
tiny pieces
i take a pen
and write myself back
into existence

- why i write

our place on earth

the universe is infinite
you are not taking up too much space
you are not a waste of breath
you are resilient
iridescent
human

- you are here because we need you

this is me
surviving
on my own
because
everyone
assumed
i would never

- appreciate doubt

our place on earth

there was a town i visited once
lonely bodies surfaced
regularly

in ditches and bars
on top of cars
in front of luxury stores

there was something rotten
about time and space

people in that town did not
subject to the rules

they did not hide
their hurt

they did not cover
their brokenness with money

blue hearts reigned
tears filled the gutters
of every home

i tried to dry my laundry
in the garden there
once

it turned rigid and froze
till this day it has not thawed

vic lejon

outsiders were scared of the town
told me not to go

you will catch your death, they said
i recounted it later as an
anecdote

try hiding invisible scars,
one of the townsman told me,
it is not easy

and i tried
and i failed

the townsman said another week,
the sad ones, they are not rational
they are scared of help, too numb,
too deep in their holes, together
we could pull them out

he was convinced
i agreed with him

a young girl was found
dead when i awoke
on my last day

i cried and the sky cried
she was pale blue like a forget-me-not,
the townspeople cried, too

our place on earth

i went to her funeral
her family liked
my mellow mood

she was a smart girl,
they told me

a fragile one but damn
she could crack a joke

now her eyes were closed

a bluebird flapped
its wings
and took refuge
from the cold winds

its feathery body
nestled
into the flowers
on top of her grave

and outsiders
call this a community
of sins, depression
scares them

- let's talk about
mental health

chapter III

can you bloom in this society
or does it stunt your growth?

vic lejon

i purged myself
of the language
which reminded me
of pain

once i was better
i learnt a part of me
had gone missing

i was speaking, talking, joking
people understood me
quite fine

but amongst the many pieces
that made up my life
i lost a part of home

the first voice
that ever lived
inside my mind

- mother tongue

our place on earth

nowadays
even getting lost
needs to be done right

     - how do i find myself?
      i ask the AI

vic lejon

infants are born
with plastic straws
in their hands

grubby and greedy
as soon as they emerge

they pierce the soil
of the earth
that birthed
them

sucking
its life-sustaining
juices
dry

to be better
than the next baby
in the crib

- how to breed selfish minds

our place on earth

the past slams its door
in my face
but i keep knocking
until splinters
dig
deep tunnels
under my skin

isn't it strange
our obsession
with would-have-been's
when all we have is
here and now

all the would-have's
and could-have's
are like drugs
addictive
bad for your heart
and lungs
mental nicotine

then the future opens
its many doors
and lures me in

- insomnia nations

i discovered
that my body
is a skilled liar

for years
it feigned fierce
protection
for the fruits
thriving
in my hips

but every month
under veiled
crimson skies (and cries)
it infused poison
into the very core
of my womanhood

all i have to show
are damaged apples and pears
serving no purpose
just dead things
woman wears

- infertility

our place on earth

society
can make you feel
like a fraud
in your own body

so whenever you can
make people feel safe
allow them
to be themselves
encourage them
to be brave

learn to co-exist
in your unique ways

- comparison crises

we tend to forget
people are entangled
with us

me, you
the person you hate

we are part of a network
called humanity

every choice we make
has an effect

every pain and ache
is felt by someone else

be it through verbal outbursts
physical violence or aggressive
silence

our actions have consequences
a society is defined by the many
and relies on every individual's
responsibility
to survive

- the modern society

our place on earth

when we talk
about forever
we want it
as soon as possible

patience is a nuisance
instant gratification
rules

we are conditioned
our hungry hands
are always reaching

starving eyes are
always bleeding
blue light

no one understands
you cannot rush
what is meant to last forever

- generational impatience

vic lejon

change is inevitable
every living being grows

do not pretend
you have not
noticed the patterns
in nature

we all become
someone else
after we have been

> hurt
> loved
> pushed
> abandoned
> judged
> hated
> ...

- *evolving*

our place on earth

high-speed trains
growing pains
a country erodes
political belly bloats
another murderous monsoon
another oil field bloom
patriotic pride pervades
common sense evades

- *current events*

vic lejon

it is in solitude
i am my truest self
and it is where i will
always return to
when i am lost

- introvert

our place on earth

when you have
judged and hurt
yourself
in every
imaginable
way

you do not
want to do
it
upon others

- they say i'm too nice/
i say that's okay

vic lejon

i have murdered
a million versions
of myself
to be
who i am
today

 - *muted murderee*

our place on earth

you claim to be
my voice of reason

(did i ever agree to that?)

my trust in you
has dwindled

we both sit
next to regret
in our beds

you say yes
when i say no

you call it democratic
i don't know

- political inertia

vic lejon

the front page news
with their pearl-white teeth

lurk on every supermarket
shelf, scheming

they want to taste your skin
test your saliva for market research

what about the truth
you may ask
can i trust their words?

not all of them, i'm afraid

the truth is hard to come by
in this mass information
day and age

- sensational!

our place on earth

we stood in lines today
towers of toilet paper
separating humans
from their common sense

and children wiped
their snotty hands
on the advertisement
for a sugar drink
(the one with artificial vitamins)

step away from strangers
cover your face
wash your hands

i am scared of this person,
snotty-hands-child whispered
and its family stepped
away from a struggling man

another example of groupthink
to be recorded in the history books

the twentysomethings pull up
next to us, they hoard all the beers

- the start of mass hysteria

vic lejon

they
pierced my tongue
with a nail gun
to mark me
as one of them

no anaesthesia
like a slaughtered cow
their fingernails dug
into my mouth
and took a shot

they towered before me
with bulging eyes
as my lips
dripped blood

i ask them, why
w h y ,   w h y ?
can't i just be me?

no.

- slaughterhouse tunes

our place on earth

every creature
we adore

we drive extinct
with great dolour

blissful blindness
to their pain

we trim our bodies
obsessively vain

feed me
groom me
focus on M-E

always taking more
unapologetically

- animal cruelty

my old self cowered
in my bedroom
when i came home
last night

she told me
about the cracks
in her self-esteem
inflicted
by society

grow a thicker skin
be more confident
stop being a girl who feels
everything

i listened to her
even though
i was her
once

and i told her,
there is a reason
we are who we are
your softness is needed
in this world

- softness

the prettiest words
will sound faint
when they fall
upon the wrong ears

- listen to understand, not to speak

remember
gestures of kindness
can be contagious
too

they can carry hope
from one mind
to another
across the entire globe

- pandemic

our place on earth

listen to the stories
the ones
eyes tell
for they
hold the secrets
how to know someone well

    - *look up*

they hired me
for pushed-up
breasts
and smooth-shaven
legs

enamoured by the fake smile
i have grown up wearing
you can no longer see the scars
from the threads inside my lips

tug up, tug down
it works like a charm

be a doll, grab me a coffee
do not defy me, i am your boss
we hired you to present
your physique not to
use the pink mass
behind your
eyes

oh, how i wish *you* would
i smell your bias from across
the room
not even aftershave can
cover it, boss

- sex doll

our place on earth

do not claim me
as yours

i am not a possession
to be passed
among men

i am a woman on a mission
and you may follow along

  - keep up (if you can)

vic lejon

first
they killed the old me

now
they want her back

dig up her body
make her look pretty

quick
quick

we do not like the new you

i smirk
because i do

- self-love

our place on earth

do not paint
a perfect picture
of others

we are humans
we make mistakes

- when life becomes an art gallery

plastic eyes
and rubber arms
their scent
like sweetened gasoline

we wander
through Synthesia
in search
of the societal dream

gobble up
foil-skinned lies
factory-made breasts
and lips

brush the rain clouds
from the sky
imperfections are tiring

sirens howl
people scram
our gummy limbs are quivering

the TV's blare
sensationalism
an old lady recounts
her teenage sins

- Synthesia, a fictional town (?)

our place on earth

before i met you
i heard the tales
of the women
you had strung along

you kept them like baubles
in a Christmas tree
for your friends
to ridicule

then you met me
were all cocky
and loud
tied a leash
around my throat

you did not see
the scissors
i kept them
hidden in my coat

i am not here
to spread my legs
i have come
to free my sisters
snip, clip, tap

- girls, support each other

vic lejon

growing up
i was never reduced
to being *just* a girl

i was never discouraged
from dirtying my hands
in the stinking mud
or rubbing shoulders
with kids who liked cars

i cried
i got angry

no emotion was off-limits
i followed others and
i led others, assertively

i learnt boys cry too
but often they were told
not to (or to hide it in the closet)

when i asked adults
why
no one could give me
a logical explanation
and to this day
i have not found one

- girls and boys

our place on earth

i used to think
the unknown
is scary

a bad place to be
because people
told me:

you need direction
you need a plan
you need a strategy

what worked
for them
did not work
for me

i thrive
in the unknown
the dark place that
scares the many
where bare feet get calloused
and bloodied

i like it there
it moulds me into the person
i always wanted to be

- fierce and free

this thing
inside my skull
will not quit
telling me
what to do
and how
to do it

it keeps
pushing me
to continue
to get better
faster
harder

bite your lips
don't mind the blood
you are here to win
do not trip up

do not disappoint me
i am you
you are here to be
the best

- perfectionist

our place on earth

i call them
drillers
the people who
have boring machines
attached to their fingers
like in-grown nails

they only reveal themselves
when they encounter
someone different
from them

you can hear them
drilling, boring and
coughing up dust
when their black-and-white
thought patterns crumble

they are desperate
to maintain
the world they have built
around them

a busy place that must be
since reality is made
of rainbow lights
erupting
from extraordinary minds

- rainbow glow

vic lejon

wooden splinters
are lodged
in a child's hand
trying
to claw
its way
out of a cage
it cannot even see

we
have put
each other
into boxes (again)
by blindly choosing
wildfire minds and
deep-frozen hearts
to lead

rhythmically
like ocean waves
we suppress the memories
passed on to us
for centuries

how much will we disrespect history
this time?

   - divisions of society

our place on earth

the newspapers
are singing in the streets

their paper bodies
are wilting in the rain
pitter-patter from digital clouds

they belt it out
in a perfect crescendo

time is dwindling
be scared of yourselves

storms
will uproot our spines

the sun
will torch our money

the oceans
will boil us alive

generation Y
will end humanity

in other news
we are building walls
and get high on toxic waste

- global anxiety

vic lejon

the past
echoes
inside our bones

the mistakes
we have made
hones our DNA

still, we commit
the same crimes
we fall
into patterns
we bite
helping hands

how do you shatter these cycles?
how do you win against egos?
how do you learn from history?

do not let the hatred win again
(please)

- blood on your hands

our place on earth

allow the youth
to write
its own story
instead of
forcing them to follow
a rotten narrative

- for the future

vic lejon

calories
age
money

there is no
perfect value

your self-worth
is not a number

you determine
who you are

- you are precious

do not force yourself
to love the sunlight

the moonlight
is just as beautiful

- your choice

vic lejon

while i cried
i began to laugh

they thought
i had gone insane
but at least
i felt alive

i wonder about them
sometimes

- who is the sane one?

our place on earth

they
ask me
what i want
to be

i don't care
ask me what i do
right now

ask me what matters
to me
and will not let me
sleep
not let me eat
forget that i need
to move
and breathe

ask me
about the things that kill me
like Bukowski put it
that is the thing i want
to talk about

i write
that is what i do

i sometimes tell them that
defying their expectations
of graceful small talk

vic lejon

and i observe
the judging frowns
etched into their bobbleheads

and sometimes
i feed them the lies
they want to hear
to please them and
pet their world-view

it is a benefit for us both
their small minds get fed
and i flex the muscles
i need for writing fiction

i am studying to become a teacher
a businesswoman
an upstanding citizen

is that what you want to hear?

yes, yes
that sounds wonderful, dear
they smile
teeth like white-picket fences

my favourite moments
occur
when i tell the truth
i am in my 20s
i don't know what i do

our place on earth

they pity me
and the ones
who raised me

for they think i am
a waste of space
but i feel great

- people-pleasing society

chapter IV

can you hear nature
through all this white noise?

we slosh around
in our mothers' bellies
like we once
dipped
and dived
through
space and time

from tiny atoms to
blushing babies
how lucky we are
to live
in sun's shine

- earthlings

our place on earth

the crocuses
daffodils
and tulips
are too tired
to rise
this spring

sunlight barely peeks
through the clouds
anymore

why should we
lift our heavy heads?

the humans barely
admire us anymore

why should we
bloom for them?

bloom for yourselves,
mother earth says

- *late spring*

vic lejon

why are compassion and kindness
difficult concepts for humans,
the moon asks

and i shrug
i do not know what to say

it costs nothing
but it gives
endlessly,
the moon continues

i could tell the moon
we choose to judge
because we envy

we choose to take
because we lack

we choose to hate
because we fear

the moon would not
understand
it sits in space
all by its lonesome
and admires our home

- *human nature*

our place on earth

people act
like we have
a planet b

pierce this one's heart
with a plastic fork
despite the warnings
of its ferocity

(storms, fires, floods, quakes)

people try it, still
they are eager
to succeed

they love their
single-use cutlery

what excitement
to unleash the anger
of the soil, skies and seas

let earth wash us away
this planet is boring
anyway

     - irritants

vic lejon

we are the people
in this beautiful hell

- *rising temperatures*

our place on earth

they swept
climate change
under the rug

trampled
spat
flattened it

like a piece of dirt
stuck to their shoes
staining their perfect
bleached lives

give it a chemical wash
repeatedly iron it

what if the rug catches fire?
i asked

it won't, little girl!
climate change is not real,
they replied

their entire
neighbourhood
burnt down
that night

- doubters

vic lejon

the Amazon,
Arctic and Australia
stand alight

smoky tendrils
decorate our skies

and people
squeeze their eyes
shut tight
hold their ears
in fright

a planet melts
like candle wax
over manicured feet

yet they rejoice
at the unusual heat

the glasses of ignorance
saddle the ridge
of their deformed noses

they snap social media sunset 'pics'
this ashy filter ruins their trips

- filter reality

earth has no ego
she is not scared to lose
that ailment is human
it created her abuse

    - ego

vic lejon

she lounges on a piano
a dingy bar
in London's bowels

the distant thunder
dances on her skin

the last hope
of humanity

what is the point
she will not sing

and the bartender
slides her another drink

thanks, darling,
she coos,
isn't life tiring?

> *- siren drowned*
> *in white noise*

our place on earth

can you feel
the heat
of burning butterfly
wings

the hymn of
bad omens
a mockingbird sings

the sense of
foreboding
the way
earth swings

its orbit has
ruptured
like vermin
we erode

big planet of earth
no longer
our abode

- kaleidoscope of butterflies

vic lejon

in my dreams
i run
from wolves

their fangs
snap at my flesh

awake
in a haze
i remember

outside live
the wolves
without teeth

inside are
the humans
smirking at me

- predators

our place on earth

if Atlas still
held earth

would his
spine
snap
from the weight

would his
palms have
searing
scars

or would he laugh
at our fate

- pollution and Greek mythology

vic lejon

i wonder
if mother earth
ever wants to undress and
wash off all the grime

take her sweeping hands
and pluck
continents from her spine

shrug off mountains
nailed to her skin
for millennia

watch them float
like a silky blouse
through space and time

stripped and raw
a body of cobalt blue
she would recover her shine

the most divine
planet home
we never saw

- *raw*

our place on earth

every star
is a reminder
of how tiny
we are
and how
beautiful
it is
that we exist
on this planet
together

- perspectives

forests, oceans and skies
hold copies of our souls
for us to come find
when we do not
feel whole

- *nature*

our place on earth

the sun sent her flowers
to tackle me

they pinned me down
with their leafy hands

whatever doubt you have
we will wash you clean

they scrubbed and rubbed
sprinkled yellow dust
along my cheekbones

kissed my forehead
and told me to run

there is so much to do
so much to see

whatever you can imagine
you can be

- sunshine human

thousands
of light-years away
lives a butterfly
constructed of stars

it is home
to souls
who were too bright
for our world

- the people we lost
(butterfly nebula)

our place on earth

i hope my tears
will feed the soil
make flowers bloom
and rain worms smile
so that even in pain
i will not be in vain

- give and take

vic lejon

when the world ends
let's watch the comets rain

hold each other's bodies
in a tight embrace

run across fields
with terror in our lungs

crying
singing

it's just a soft apocalypse
it's just another beginning

- pastel demise

our place on earth

they tell me
i cannot save
every sad soul
i meet

it will tire me out
drain the energy
from my bones

you would think
compassion is finite

we run on oil
what irony

there is no proof
for your assumption
just your fear of sincerity

i recommend you try
this foreign concept
of empathy

that energy you are scared
of losing, it refills

how is that for
a marketing strategy?

- free refills

vic lejon

i forgot to water
the house plant
again

it dropped another leaf
for me to clean up

i'm sorry
little one
i am trying
i told it one night

and it shook its little arms
till they were bare
looked up at me
and said

water yourself
human
i can smell your despair

- listen to your house plant

our place on earth

flowers
wither in winter
to bloom again
in spring

trees grow
and shed leaves
to produce
oxygen

we buckle
in times of struggle
to become better versions
of ourselves

    - cycles

stuck in a dreary world
with insistent
insecurities
and decay

i imagine a life
in harmony

where sunshine
creates
pastel skies
every day

parks are filled
with cherry trees
and blushing cheeks
couples on first dates

a world where humans
cross sugar bridges
together, instead of
barricading them

value each other's
differences
and always have
hands to hold

- hoping for utopia

our place on earth

when i was little
i fell asleep
with a globe
in my arms

no concept of earth's
significance
to me, to us

she gives us air
water, soil
and warmth

we trust her every night
when we go to bed
and wake up
in the morning

a little older
a little wiser
a little more scared
of the day
she turns her back
on us

- mama earth

vic lejon

i keep an urn
on my window sill
it is unused as of yet

it serves as a reminder
in times i feel ill
that our world will come
to an end

what is more powerful
than a mindset of doom?

a constant nag in your brain
that no matter how harsh
or polluted your tongue
angst and hysteria
are in vain

twirl your hair and thumbs
stuff your belly with spice
humanity has long ago
decided to roll its dice

we scored a snake eye
bit into the apple of greed
and purged each other
of empathy

our place on earth

animals are our feed
kiss our feet
you are weak

forests are broccoli
free to boil and fry
lather them in butter
i despise the green taste

yet mother earth spins
caught in its wheel
electrified by humanity
and its technologies

move to a virtual world
the sunlight is brighter
full saturation, full contrast
nothing has consequences

remember the urn?
this is what it says

people will lose
their homes (and lives)
fields will scorch
creatures will starve
polar ice caps will fall

vic lejon

when you walk amongst
the seven billion
think about your existence
and the future anxiety

consider what your
children's children
would give for
your carefree life

instead of uncertainties
let us fill the empty urn
with wishes of how
we want to be

we want to be compassionate
we want a peaceful home
we want to be happy
and see our children full-grown

we want a healthy planet
now that will take time
but if we do this together
we will extend our lives

- open your eyes

if every thought
was an infinitesimal
scripture engraved
onto your bones

what would you say?
what would you hope?

_____

_____

_____

_____

_____

_____

_____

_____

- to be read by future generations

vic lejon

for the future of earth,
for the future of humanity,

a brave girl shouts

- why does the youth revolt?

our place on earth

no matter what you go through
you are never alone on earth

    - community

destruction
always leaves
something behind

the chance
for something
new

while old flowers
bloomed
for the sun

the new ones
will feed
on the moon

- evolution

our place on earth

in times of uncertainty
we tend to forget
that the world
keeps improving

it is the tiny changes
that cause the biggest effects

a butterfly flapping
its wings
a child sitting
by the sea

the motion is
too minuscule
for you and i to see

impossible to
put into words

close your eyes
and listen
you can hear
mother earth
brim with hope

- trust

vic lejon

our place on earth

thank you for spending
your time and attention
on my words.

i hope they brought you
inspiration, understanding
and made you reflect.

be kind,
be well.

- vic lejon

our place on earth

for book updates, poetry and prose
follow vic on instagram

@vic.l.poetry

if you enjoyed this book, please consider
sharing it with your family and friends.
leave a review. hide it under someone's
pillow. wrap it as a present.

independent authors always appreciate
your support.

CPSIA information can be obtained
at www.ICGtesting.com
Printed in the USA
BVHW072306101121
621198BV00003B/362